ABSTRACT

Obscurity of Life is a collection of Poetry written over a period of time and experiences in real life. The book talks about Love, Women, Social Causes, Nature, Life and Death.

Ajeesh Venugopalan

First edition 2020

The Author has made every effort to trace and acknowledge sources/resources/individuals. In the event that any images/information have been incorrectly attributed or credited, the Author will be pleased to rectify these omissions at the earliest opportunity.

ISBN 978-81-936602-9-4

Published by Author's Channel, # 108, 1st floor, 3rd cross, 3rd stage, 8th Main, Pillana Garden Lingarajapurm, Bangalore 560045

Printed and bound in India by Thomson Press India Ltd.

AUTHOR'S CHANNEL

http://authorschannel.in/

To my darlings Lakshmi and Prarthana

ACKNOWLEDGMENT

With the deepest gratitude, I thank my parents Shri. C. Venugopal and Mrs. Ambujam for bringing me into this world and their never-ending support in the making of me; what I am today is all because of their efforts in constantly moulding me. My Wife, Remya for living through my madness every day. My brother, Vineesh for always being a devil's advocate and helping me perfect the craft.

I would like to acknowledge and express my gratitude to my friends; Jose, Sajin and Srikkanth for leading my memoir back to our classroom bench where it all started as casual musings. Their encouragement has motivated me to do better. Two great buddies Ram and Aneesh for being with me throughout. All my teachers for their inspirational teachings. To all the writers and creative professionals in the world, who has touched my heart. Finally, my darlings Lakshmi and Prarthana.

I would also like to thank my Publisher Aruna Naidu for her guidance. Anoop Alexander and Merril Anil for their marvellous cover design. I wish to thank every person who came into my life and enlightened me through their presence.

Obscurity of Life

Contents

Section 1: Love

BIRTH

Oust. I first bumped against a little young tadpole after I was set free. He looked a bit lost in the obscurity of life. Neither of us knew how to swim, and we were contemplating our first move, that's when several other tadpoles like him and I were showered on us like a midnight summer rain. Hot; fresh and burning. My little tail got entangled with a few other tadpoles; the only arm I had then, which allowed me to swim. Without wasting a moment, I untangled my tail and swam in search of love. Swimming came to me naturally when I tried.

I then swam against all the odds, massive tides and outperformed a million others like me to find my princess. When I saw her, we embraced each other and fused into one like fog and then got lost in the dreams of eternity. I, the little young tadpole, will never be the same again. I have amalgamated with my princess to become one life and lost in love forever to begin yet another one. Little about 8 millimetres in size and the deepest and darkest place in the womb, I rose again on the 36th day, made of gold, silver, and light, I shimmered red beams to spread the rays of love. I am the heart, presenting to you Obscurity of Life.

My fate was locked when an astrologer made his prediction in 2003, that I will not find my love because I had Ketu in the fourth house of my birth chart. However, I wonder, stay awake in the late hours of the night in anxiety and ponder to find new ideas to overpower the Ketu, defeat him and conquer every other heart in this world. Since then I have been spreading the red beams in the hope of finding waves of love; reciprocate and rejoice in the search for the like-minded. My understanding of love evolved, and it transpired to its current state, which may not yet be perfect.

Love could be amorous madness during adolescence allowing testosterone to gush through your testicles or ovaries on the first sight of the opposite gender. For most, it occurs during school, and the case was not different for me as well. The only true physical contact one has with the mother through the umbilical cord. Caressing; a touch of fondness by the parents fades as we grow. After puberty it is felt as sexually obstructive; however unintended it becomes circumspect. The child inside one still misses the tender love offered to him or her by the parent.

Love

"If love is like a lonely walk in the rain,
If love is the cure for all your pain
And if in love you have so much to gain,
Then Why, Why does love go in vain."

Thanks to my good friend Sajin for being an inspiration.

Repent

Please forgive me,
For I have plucked you off your root,
Once for my girl.
Oh my little Lotus,
Did you curse me then?
I did not find her even today.

My Cereus

Several flowers had bloomed in my garden,
All faded and died with time.
During the prolonged darkness of the past,
None had spread its fragrance.
Now the moment has come,
For My Cereus to bloom and stay,
Forever and ever...

Seeking Love

As the night falls, I try to sleep
Soaked in my own tears,
Waiting for the sun to rise,
Bringing new hope,
That again fades off with the day.
Your searing memories
Makes my life more bitter,
But still I yearn
To find a little space,
In your big heart.
With shattered dreams and solitude
Standing out among the crowd
Thoughts being mesmerized
I recollect the past.
Future being so uncertain
Still being optimistic
I still yearn for your love,
May I get it from earth?
Or may I get it from heaven

My Lost Heart

Amidst toil and tiresome labour
I know not to remember,
When I got lost in love.
In search of my forgone heart,
I linger and loiter.
And off loaded my emotions,
On finding it in you.

My love now so deep,
Make my life still so dun.
The gut that's inside of me and,
Your semblance drives me dotty.

My minion, I love to
Tell you one a thing.
Shoot my heart
To umpteen pieces.
But help me gather, and
Make them whole with
Your sweet kisses!

Within me!

Let your heart beat in mine;
Though miles away, yet fine.
Whirled in duty and time,
Yet cuddled within me.
Wish I could forever see,
Hear you like a bumble bee
Within me!

In the sky shall I take wings?
To fly and breathe into your lungs.
God forbid unforeseen instance lest,
Tie me down to the beats in your chest.
Your soul shall I shadow,
Hug you at all the meadow;
Within me!

Your feet, the land it touch,
Flowers shall in the green pastures bloom.
Your beauty and love is such,
Pull you out whilst misery and gloom;
For you shall live in me and me in you;
For we are among the blessed lot a few
Within me!

Made for each other

Drowned in the ocean of love,
I call my love for rescue.
Where she pretends to be deaf,
Denies mercy
And the quest continues.
It's no fancy or fantasy
For love shall not fail
Let me wait for your mail
Which showers on me
With your thoughts,
So fine and sweet.

Drowned in the ocean of love,
I call my love for rescue.
Pretend not to be blind,
For I shall give you
Thousand reasons, to tell you, that love is supreme
And will remain so
For another thousand seasons,
Yet to come.

Drowned in the ocean of love,
I call my love for rescue.
Pretend not to be dumb;
Utter the word love,
To find this world so beautiful.
Let us enjoy the legacies of God together. He only says,
We are made for each other.

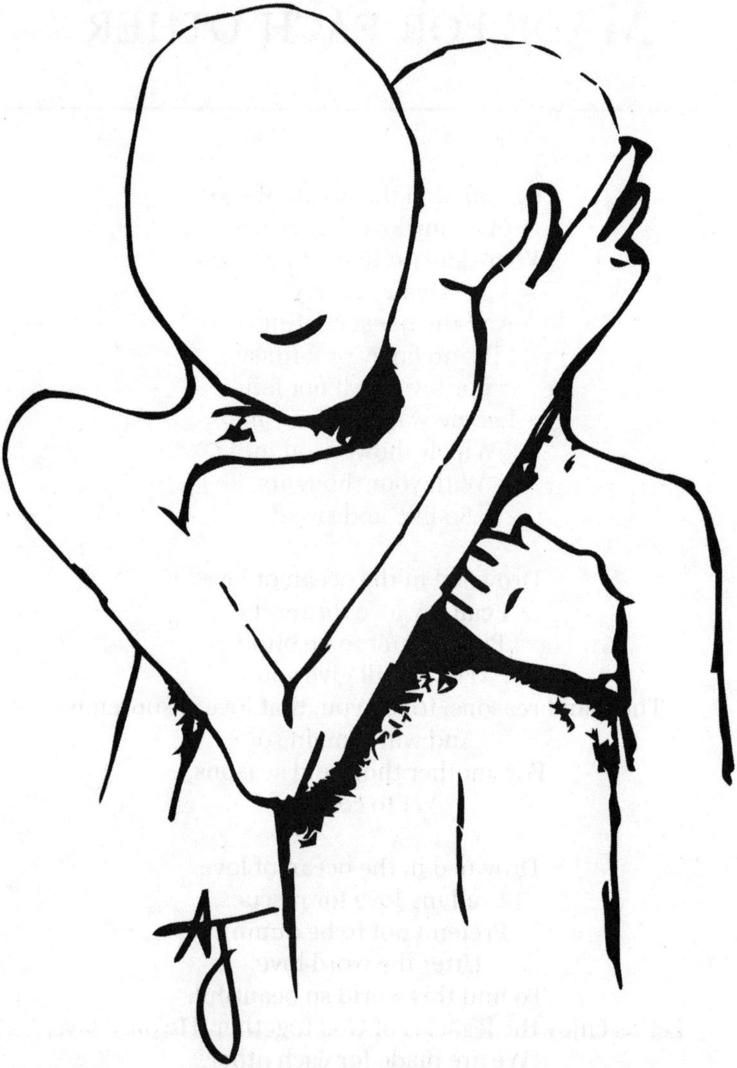

PRISONER FOR LIFE

Every a time I retaliate with my own inner self,
I throw you away
With immense force.
But each time you surfaced again and stick on to me
Like a parasite,
To quench the thirst for love.
It's been years;
Fighting against my destiny, I know not
How long to wait;
Or shall I become extinct before.
I am prisoned for life. The prison of Love

True Love

You broke my heart,
To umpteen pieces.
I shall regret not,
For I have loved you
Once and forever.

My soul will leave the body,
On your wedding day.
The church bells may sing,
A wedding song for you.
Your husband may garland you,
And you may garland him in turn.

My body will await you,
In the cemetery behind.
My body will await you,
To garland it.

Please shed one drop a tear,
Before my body is buried.
My soul will await you, up in the heaven,
For one simple reason that;
I love you.

Adieus

Every morning; I greet you morning;
But you seem to be lost in the net.
I wait for your greeting,
But your reply is pending yet.
I know not to hate
May you find your mate;
Before it's too late.
But don't take a decision in haste.
I am just an old friend stopped by to say Adieus.
I leave Bangalore for pay.
Just smile and say hey;
Before my hair turn grey.
I wait for your greeting,
But your reply is pending yet.
If you are so busy,
Thinking fussy!
Let me say bye forever.
Will come in your way never.
I am just an old friend stopped by to say,
Adieus, I leave you forever.

A LITTLE SMOKE FOR MY SOUL

A little smoke for my soul,
While others are lucky to be in group,
And when tears touch down my feet;
I break down! And then I need;
A little smoke for my soul.

Strange are the ways of solitude,
Sometimes beautiful, sometimes grieving, sometimes lost in thought and
Sometimes I need;
A little smoke for my soul.

In the midst of my life,
I was enticed with the first feeling of love,
But then when I lost her,
I need, a little smoke for my soul.

I envy others in group,
And when my heart goes with the group,
Then, then I need a little smoke for my soul,
A little smoke for my soul.

Impossible Aspirations

Nothing in this world is mine,
but everything is fit and fine.
The beauty of a rose, I adore,
Faded and died when tried to explore.
Now, I understand it was never mine.
Nothing in this world is mine,
but everything is fit and fine.

The legacy I got from forefathers;
was spent in no time.
Now I understand it was never mine.
Nothing in this world is mine,
but everything is fit and fine.

She was beautiful from heart,
and I lost control over mine.
But before I could own her,
I understood she was never mine.
Nothing in this world is mine,
but everything is fit and fine.

YOU, I AND THE WEB

I know now, the enlightening truth.
Bitter still digestive,
Thirsty intestines have been looking for you.
Long time now, still I wish if you were the one.
The one and only one made for me.
The search continues in desperation.
Wow, the technology has embodied.
Now I have the web to cluster my interests.
Still immature, it just couldn't get the right match.
I wish if it could peak into the hearts of the millions,
And find the synergy in you and I.
I know now, the enlightening truth.
Ah match making is complex.
The stupid heart broods, 28 years and counting.

Love Is Wife

Meaning of the word,
Penned and told by several men,
They fought for with their mighty sword,
The Princess of Troy or Love.
I understand it better.

I got married and it's a while now.
She showers a lot of love.
Meaning of the word love,
Stands incomplete without her.
Yes, I understand it better and
The meaning of the word love is wife.

Section 2: Apple of your eye

Mrs Iyer

It's true that the greatest realization comes in the absence of what you are seeking and in the presence of exuberating pain. When you have all your organs functioning properly no one ever bothers to take care of them. That's the same case with me and few of the people I have known.

When I received a missed call, I flipped my phone around to see that it was from Mrs. Lakshmi Subramanium Iyer. The first time I answered her missed call with a call, I thought that the old lady may not have enough balance in her cell phone. Two days later, I received yet another missed call from her. This time around I waited for few minutes before I gave her a call back. The next day again I received another missed call and so it continued. Every time she gave me a missed call, I returned the call and talked to her for long hours.

Sometimes I complained to my friend Raj, that his mom gave me missed calls too many times. "Why don't you ask her to give me a call?" Raj used to say that he would recharge her prepaid connection when he would go back. Yes, Mrs. Lakshmi Subramanium Iyer is my best friend's Mother. Back in those good old college days, she used to serve food for all of us; including me, Raj, Anil, Harsha, Manoj and many other infrequent visitors to Raj's house. Her "Vatha Kolombu" (a very special Tamil style curry) is my favourite. Every time I visit her, I request her to prepare this curry for me and it is the best "Vatha Kolombu" I have ever had anywhere in Tamil Nadu.

Most of the time, she would talk to me about Raj and his indifferent attitude towards her, for he was in love with a Punjabi kudi. Of course it was a very difficult relationship; for the state of Punjab to unite with the state of Tamil Nadu. It created problems in both their families. The phone calls continued and every time the call ended with a note of promise from me, to talk to Raj and have him back off from the relationship. As per my promise, I did speak to Raj, but it was in vain. He was still so madly, deeply in love and was very determined to marry the Punjabi kudi. Mrs. Lakshmi Iyer even had agreed to their relationship once because she wanted to see her son married before she succumbed to the Cancer. Cancer had re-appeared in her after two and half years and this time around it had spread into the bone marrow, liver and her lungs. The doctors had already warned the family. Those of us who knew of it, kept her in ignorance as she would panic at death being so very close; and one that is inevitable. On the other hand, the girl's family was not ready to move with this relationship and as such the relationship never really worked out.

I stopped complaining about the missed calls, for I knew that sooner or later I would stop receiving those missed call. The last time I spoke to her, she told me that all her kids are married; with kids and happily settled in life. A few drops of tears dripped down my cheek. I cried.

I have stopped receiving those missed calls since December 2009. During her last days, she was too weak to pick up the phone and give a call by herself. January 11th 2010 she left this world. Since then I honestly do long for those precious missed calls, which I know will never come.

I miss you Mrs. Lakshmi Subramanium Iyer and so does Raj. Raj remains unmarried. Still determined to marry his love, but yes a feeling of guilt sometimes gushes through his nerves. But Mrs. Lakshmi Subramanium Iyer had already seen her kids married and settled in her dreams. Some dreams are never fulfilled and so do some missed calls I complained about will never be seen on my cell phone again. It's true that the greatest realization comes in the absence of what you are seeking for and in the presence of exuberating pain.

Legacy of a Mom

Thou pretty daughter,
So tender and delicate,
Fed and nurtured with care,
Resembled a sculpture,
Carved out of a stone,
By thou own hands.
She, she is the legacy of a mom.

Thy pretty daughter,
Married off to a doctor,
Renowned by his fame,
Showered her with red roses,
The symbol of love.

Later she puked.
Thou pretty daughter,
Carried for nine months,
To find her sibling,
With crippled legs
And an insane mind.
Carved out of a stone,
By thou own hands,
She, she is the legacy of a mom.

Furious and callous,
The doctor failed.
Thou pretty daughter,
Back home she sailed.
Struck by misery,
Time failed to heal the wound.
Thou pretty daughter,
So tender and delicate,
Trembled to death.

Thou pretty daughter,
With crippled legs
And an insane mind,
Survives still, for
She, she is the legacy of a mom.

GRANNY

On the bed, I lay
Remembering that forgone day,
Looking at her wrinkled cheek
And hands so sleek,
She fed me milk with.

Like a stone dropped in a pond, her naval.
Like the tides generated, her belly.
I sleep on her lap then.

Lullabies she sung,
Melodious they were.
Stories she narrated,
Remains still in memory,
Frozen and so fresh.

Innocence of her grandchild,
She liked so much.
Snatching away the innocence,
She liked so much,
Time had changed.

The child had grown.
Old and pale the granny
In the village so far
Waits still to find,
Her grandson,
Lost in the concrete jungle.

Mother who oozes Blood

A wave of responsibility gushes through me,
Just now; I heard that big news.
I tend to recollect all those mistakes from the past.
Sure to experience them again from my infant.
Your second childhood along with yours',
Teaching them the rhymes,
Picking up all that I have missed out to,
Enhance better living for the one yet to come.

It trickled through my nerves,
Fear, fear of the world so naive,
People who fight for nothing, kills for currency
And lives for blood,
Have I just sown a seed to face the bitter world?
Or was it just lust?
Counting on my wallet I am not eligible,
For the big leap, however the mistake has already been done.

Cover up the same with another one.
Have her take a pill and make the kill.
Kill that one before it's born.
Let that one be lucky not to see
This place so naïve.

The mother, who oozes blood;
Expelling the foetus, a drop of tear shed,
In tribute to a life saved from the sufferings,
Widely spread across in this rat race.
A drop of tear shed,
In tribute to a life saved.

Kid

I wish; if I was a kid,
Gone are those days,
Merry and Joy;
Seems way far still.
I have hugged,
Toilsome labour and pain;
Gone are those days,
Ice creams and lollipops;
Melted with time.
I wish; if I was a Kid,
Gone are those days,
Toys and pots;
Not to be seen.
I have loved,
Games and sleep;
Gone are those days,
Not to return for life.
I wish; if I was a kid.

TRULY YOURS

Twenty four hours a day,
Seven days a week and
Three sixty five days a year,
I was taken care by her,
So tender and delicate.

She empties a bowl of love on me,
Every second she lives.
I grew up in your arms
And so mom
I am truly yours.

Now; when I am a man, I met her.
Even without my knowledge,
I let lose my heart.
Fascination slowly tuned into love;
And now; my love
I am truly yours.

My mom's dream world
Did not allow trespassers.
I have to make a sacrifice
Either my mom or my love.
Put into a dilemma;
Lost in the world of thoughts,
Calling my lord for rescue.
I know not to betray,
Either my mom or my love;
And so my lord; I am truly yours.

My Father

Wonderful tales that my father told,
Had he not grown pale and old;
I would still have had a lot to learn.
I wonder; what I did wise and earn,
But I still; yearn for his caressing touch,
And lay my head to rest on his lap on a couch.

The power of words; which he did pass on,
Through me the world would know,
Because of him; I did grow strong,
For he is still brawn and well on.
His heart and will; cut as a sword,
With mighty words like a musical chord.

Measure not the wealth, he was poor.
He did not own coins made of gold;
But did bask in the glory grandeur.
Such is his might manifold
For he is my father, the heavens bow!
I shall too, in the blossoms of thy bough.

Section 3: Woman

Souparnika Foeticide

This story begins at a familiar but still strange colony, far away from home. I am not quiet sure about the name of this colony. But each and every building block of those houses looked so familiar to me. I tried to re-call the location but have been very unsuccessful in doing so.

I walked along those streets as if I was walking in the past, probably in the late eighties or early nineties. If this were to be a movie, it would have been portrayed in black and white or Eastman colour. My destination was a familiar house, which was again triggered from a long lost memory. I was quite sure about who I was visiting there. After reaching at the door, I found it wide open. I did not show the courtesy to knock on the door or call out for someone; I just walked in and headed directly to the master bedroom only to find a woman lying on the bed and helpless. She was a little above her middle age probably in her late thirties and nine months' pregnant, ready to give birth to a baby girl.

Now that's amazing! How do I Know a baby girl was to be born? I asked myself. I scratched my head, stressed my brains, concentrated at a pin point to find out the answer to my own question. How did I know that it's a baby girl?

But I am very sure that it's a baby girl. It is definitely a baby girl. I was confident about it, but doubted my source of confidence. While I was pondering on the source of my confidence, the lady went into labour. The baby would be born any moment now, yet the man of the house hadn't returned yet. He had been out for some reason.

It had started to rain cats and dogs sometime after I had walked into the house. I walked out again trying to hail a taxi or some sort of public transport, as I needed to get the lady to the hospital soon. She was so close to my heart that I just had to do it. Her contractions increased as I managed to hail a taxi and help her to get to the hospital.

At the hospital, the doctors and the attenders rushed her to the labour room. As the doctor was rushing her inside, I remember I was calling out:

Doctor: It's a baby girl.

You should say this is stranger than fiction! This time around I even know her name. I again call out:
Doctor: It's her Souparnika. Souparnika is going to be born.

While the woman is in the process of getting the most divine job of her life done, I started fighting with my sixth sense yet again. I had just read in books about the sixth sense, which was being experienced by the so called me.

Meanwhile her man arrives at the hospital. The neighbours had updated him about what had happened in his absence. I gave him a big hug and said:

It's a baby girl. Souparnika is going to be born.
He looked at me and smiled.

After the struggle of about few minutes the doctor's came out.

Congratulations! It's a baby girl.

I was happier than both the parents not because my sixth sense was right. I knew it was Souparnika and Souparnika is so special for me. Yes, Souparnika is born finally.

Two days later: As a result of a panic wave in the city we had to evacuate it and flee to my brother's place. I am not sure where his house is, I just know that we had to take a flight or a train to get there and that he is waiting for us there.

At the train station, the woman had trouble holding her 2 day old baby and simultaneously managing her luggages. I was young and could not help her with the luggages but I wanted to hold her: Souparnika. I offered a helping hand to the woman but she was reluctant to handover her two day old baby girl to a young boy like me. But I desperately wanted to hold Souparnika. I started fighting with the lady and touched her.

As my hands touches her soft body. She calls me by my name: Ajeesh

Oh holy god! A two day old baby girl has just called out my name. How did she know my name? And how did a 2 day old baby speak?

In fear and panic I withdrew my hands from her. Again she calls out: Ajeesh

I was scared and ran towards man who was standing a little away, reading a news paper.

I ran faster than ever calling out:

Father she calls me Ajeesh, Father she calls me Ajeesh...I am in total panic and start fighting with him and that's when I wake up from my sleep. I opened my eyes and realized that it was just a dream and just then I realized that the woman in the dream was my mom, the man was my father and Souparnika was my little sister.

Many Souparnikas are being killed in the womb all over the world. Souparnika could have been my sister or your sister, someone's mother, somebody's wife or could even have been a mother for all like Mother Teresa. This was an earnest endeavour to capture my dream, but in the process, it turned out to be a message. I hope this will capture the interest of the readers. Even today in India there are millions of female foeticide and let this be a dedication to those sad mothers.

Let us not kill yet another Souparnika.

Ordeal of a Rose

The rose as beautiful as a rose,
The rose that blooms on touch,
So tender and delicate.
The rose that stood in solitude,
The rose with immense ordeal.
The rose that strived to live.
Bad time had fallen upon her...
A brazen storm of agony tore of her petals,
Making her stand nude.
She was then raped...
She was then raped twice, thrice...

Now that the storm has passed by;
The greatest healer of wound,
Could not give her cloths.
The rose that blooms on touch
So tender and delicate.
The rose that stood nude
Now on touch; she shrink of abash.
With abated strength,
The rose that stood nude.
The rose that stood,

In the fountain of tears
Looking back into the past,
In despair, with a feeling of impending doom.
The rose that stood nude,
The rose that pounds for love;
The rose with immense ordeal,
Now she shall incarnate into a new life.
The rose that blooms on touch;
So tender and delicate.

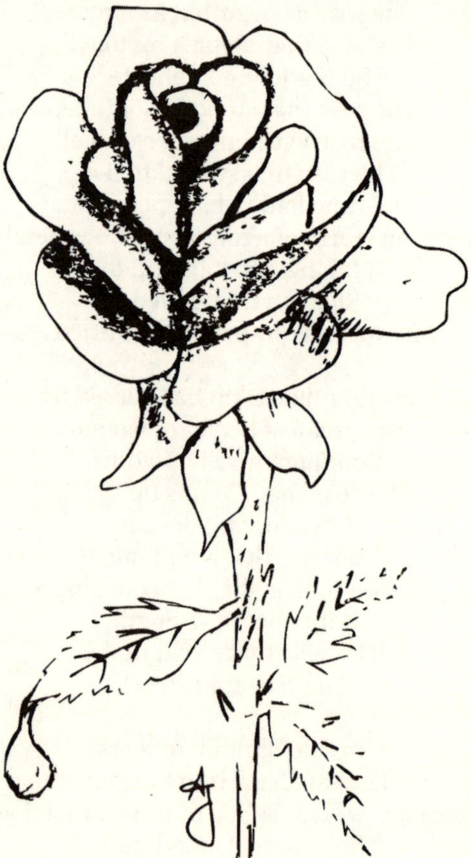

MAYA

Never been loved or nurtured,
In the world so furious,
I remain in the dungeon captured.
People around so curious,
To satisfy their lust,
I fall prey to these civilized beasts.
Thy sucking left and right my breasts.
I have never known sanctity.
Lying on the bed, my legs spread,
They over power me;
The dominating breed of thee.
Now Who am I?
I was the Bar Dancer – Maya. But Now,
I belong to the red streets.

GODDESS OF THE MOON

Be my side through the night,
For your compassion and glory remains,
You will stay the queen in our hearts so might;
Like the blood in our veins.

Be my side through the night,
Like the goddess of the moon.
You sprout a smile being in our sight,
Like the world's only boon.

Your caressing touch threw the pain away,
For you have the heart full of mercy,
Be my side through the time of day,
Like the sun so bright; praise worthy.

Be my side through the day,
The lovely fruit of grace;
With much tribulation your stay
Knocked on the heavenly space.

A rendezvous with the holy tragedy,
Made millions mourn in anguish.
You will stay the queen in our hearts so might;
Like the blood in our veins.

Be my side in the skies,
Like the only star of love,
Shower unto earth, when it cries,
Compassion and love from above.

Be my side through the night,
Like the goddess of the moon.
You sprout a smile being in our sight,
Like the world's only boon.

Lotus! My Mother

Against odds, she bloomed in slush,
Swirl of her light pink petals blossom,
Delightfully to shield me in ample and lush;
While I lay asleep in her squishy bosom.

Your majestic beauty serene and divine,
Thou name symbolic to the creator, the sun,
For you belong to the golden shrine,
In my heart; for, I being your treasured son.

You caressed me like a crystal droplet,
Strolled alongside during weathering storms,
In the water you stood like the goblet;
Yet not drenched or hurt by thorns.

She let's not ever; my life in shambles,
Her heart mighty old, but is made of gold;
Whispers wisdom in my ear and sing unto my soul,
Unlearnt; for she shall not once gamble,
With love cos there are several stories untold,
Etched in sweat and blood, that makes me whole.

Amid the call for duty towards the land,
I think off you in glee and revering memoir,
Frozen in my heart and soul, in grand.
Thus is the power of your love choir,
Rumbling inside me, keeps me awake just.
For I shall stay in your arms a must,
For you are my mother, for you are my Lotus,
For you are Ambujam.

Empty Soul

An Empty soul and a mind
Moonlit night and some wind
Sway thy emotions stream;
Till the poet commence to dream.
A long stretch on the freeway
Beautiful farms on the horizon,
With the woman on the side,
Makes it worth a romantic ride;
Only for the world to impart,
The secret of Romancing as an art!
She is carved with a purpose,
Glorious is her creator unsurp us
For she induces love with her eyes
And let my heart melt like an ice
For she is an empty soul.

Why do man love a woman?

Why do man love a woman?
So much, beyond himself
He comes from her inside,
And so does he want to return to her.
Probably return to the inside of her.

For he looks strong and tough,
All peripheral showbiz that is.
Reality! He is fragile and weak within.
He feels safe and cosy in her bosom
And weep like a baby once again.

O Beauty! Who gave you these?
Breasts, too seductive lover of lust
Feed the thirsty, the helpless man
Thy drank left and right to quench,
The everlasting illusion of thirst.

Does it really? The craving for love deepens,
Even when his arms wrap around you
His heart pressing yours in love
Even when the stench of his mouth is felt in yours
The lust for love making is never ending.

Days pass by quick, as the fluttering birds in the sky
How passionately did they mate irretrievably?
Is that just his love for your physique?
He feels your heart beat, even when he is away
Because he loves you not just for once.

Look at him for hours, instead; the mirror.
Ah you will admire it too, how worthy to be praised
A wondrous sight, you will stand still so amazed
Now you know why do man love a woman?
For his love is Eternal and not just momentary.

Section 4: Life

My Vishukani

The Marking of Auspicious beginnings in a new year starts with a Vishu Kani. On the day of Vishu every year there is an early wake up call, as early as 3 or 4 in the morning. As a young boy, I could never have my regular hours of sleep the night before Vishu. I would lay on bed fantasizing the morning Kani, Kai-neettam and fire crackers. The first kaineettam of the day is received from the eldest member of the family, after getting a blind escort with the support of a thooku vilakku (Hanging Lamp) to the neatly arranged Kani in your pooja room.

As a kid, through the gaps of those wrinkled old fingers which covered my eyes, I would take a naughty peek through to get a glimpse of her; through the light shades of the Thooku Vilakku, even before she could get me to the pooja room. Her smell refuses fade; or may be the feel of her from me or may be her existence in me.

My earliest memories of my grandmother go back to one such Vishu day; the time and the visual is frozen in the neural network of my brain, making her the one; “My Vishukani”. The Vishukani marks the beginning of a new year, but for me it marked the beginning of a new life which indeed was gifted by her; in a way.

Having mothered eight children, 4 boys and 4 girls; she survived 87 dark long years amongst all other odds. The prayer that was a part of the Eulogy for her:

“In sure and certain hope of the resurrection to eternal life through our Lord Jesus Christ, we commend to Almighty God: (C Madhavi). We commit her body to the ground; earth to earth; ashes to ashes, dust to dust. The Lord bless her and keep her, the Lord maketh his face to shine upon her and be gracious unto her and give her peace. Amen."

After three days, the fire in the cremation pyre died out, and cooking resumed at home; but the ashes were still hot. In the ashes, there was a metal ball from her hip replacement surgery and another piece of steel from when she had broken her hand. That eulogy prayer, written long ago – how true; the almighty refused to accept metal as her body parts. Let the visuals of those ashes die with me, powerful to keep you awake the whole night and scribe these lines.

She had undergone surgery for throat cancer thrice. All three times, she fought bravely for life and she indeed succeeded. Survived by eight children; today they need her legacy to be partitioned.

On the bed, I lay
Remembering those forgone days,
Her lullabies reverberating in my sensual ears;
Loud sound of those fire crackers; burst during Vishu. On the other side, I hear a shameful fight for; the legacy of a mom.

But the real legacy has been "My Vishukani". She passed away on the 26th February, 2014 (Aged: 87).This is a Tribute to C Madhavi Amma; my grandmother one of the bravest woman I have known on the occasion of this women's day. Written on the occasion of women's day in 2014.

JOURNEY

The engine spitting carbon black smoke
Carrying along thousands of folks
Some towards their home
A few to their office.
The train whistled off!

LIFE

Life may be tough, tougher or toughest
But do not concede defeat,
Retaliate with all your might and power
And gain the reins of life
Taste it with salt and pepper
Sometimes bitter, sometimes sour,
But when you are really weak to fight back,
Trust me; there is always a shoulder to lean on...

Traumatic Mind

Fallen prey to my exotic thoughts
Like a butterfly trapped,
In the venomous spider web;
Waiting to be chained and caned.
Perception differs and so am I.
Insane am I or you or the world.
To unfold this enigma,
I have been trying, causing;
Reason for the world to oust me.

Walked halfway through,
I find myself lost in the
Journey of life.
Let me ink down
For the rest to read and follow
The only justice to be done
At thou sole discretion.

Chewed and spitted I lay on thou hands
For mercy to be showered upon
Insane am I or you or the world
Or have I
Fallen prey to my exotic thoughts.

Bhavati Biksham Dehi

It was thus broken, the chatra!
Mr. Macaulay did it all.
His footing on this land;
Divine and rich with knowledge beyond life and death.
Dating 1835, the mutilation was afar any reforms.
Further did he curse, defined illegal the great services rendered,
With new laws of the brit, blind folded we follow to date
Bhavati Biksham Dehi is reinvented as the loan.
Money and materialism; are sheer human inventions.
The wrath of the, then Acharya commune
Loiter around the space, traveling back and forth in time
Poet Hafez you pinned it once
A humble soul like me would do nothing
But reiterate to this world;
Those beautiful words you uttered once.
And still, after all this time,
The sun never says to the earth,
"You owe me."
Look what happens with a love like that,
It lights the whole sky.
Such was the unconditional love
Limitless compassion of great teachers
Let me remain a humble seeker of Knowledge
Indoctrinate me as a Brahmin! A true one.
Would remain a receiver in kind
Your unconditional love and limitless compassion
Bhavati Biksham Dehi
May you give me some alms?
Bhavati Biksham Dehi

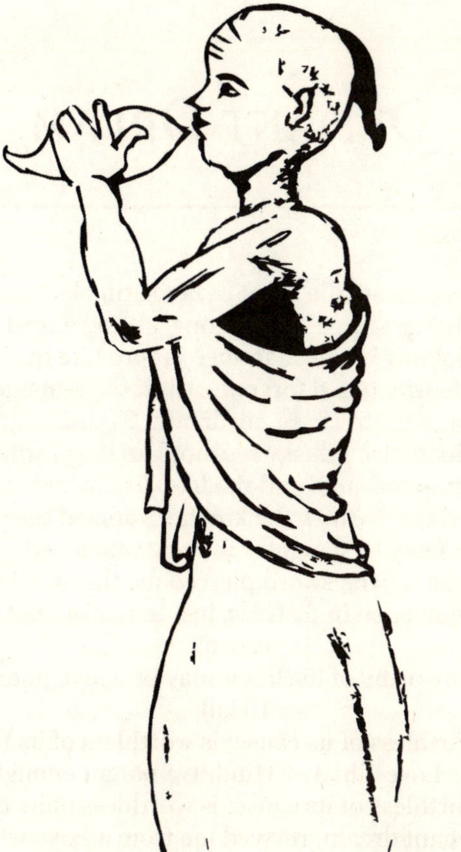

Defiant Dream

I eloped on a horse; the scent of her satin blew up in the air;
While she galloped along; sitting ahead.
The stroke of her flesh induced more Life in to mine;
The Life which had forgone ordeal of great confines;
In conquest to chase my dream; Swords spit fire;
Shed blood, deep dusky red-hot like the erupted lava.
Esteem stood high and the blood splashed further;
From dawn to dusk the knights pursued the chase.
Only to slaughter the one who loved.
When finally the sword pierced me through I rouse!
My eyes wide open in distress, just to realize that was just a dream.
A dream unworthy of itself; Or may be a love potent enough to kill;
Is worthless of its cause; is worthless of its time.
Jihad or Love Jihad or Hindutva potent enough to kill
Is worthless of its cause; is worthless of its time.
A defiant dream, revived me from a Love which,
Is worthless of its cause; is worthless of its time.

Displaced

In our own land, when we become a nomad,
Destitute of land, stolen the home had,
By the self-proclaimed democratic rulers,
Winning the votes of thy own farm producers.

Their tiring feet walks past woods a several miles,
In search of tranquillity and a new utopia;
Vowed under the declaration for ten deciles,
But finally put to rest in the realms of myopia.

The promise of loan waiver, I wonder!
Under the contracts of wide blue yonder;
Reality struck when they run-down of water,
And suffer in the dark hours of night in hunger.

Erected dams in the name of irrigation,
The land then hawked, belongs for agriculture.
Corporates encumber those in invasion,
To erect concrete tower seeking candidature.

A few among the displaced souls then made slaves,
With permanent stature in concrete caves;
Thus widen gaps between the rich and the poor,
Corporates then offer them alms in grandeur.

Silenced

Rogues of the land, power in thou hands by addiction,
Arrest Kṛṣṇá the prince, the lord! Under sedition,
For only having spoken in favour of solidarity,
A remonstration in silence broke for popularity.

Like the falling pen mighty; when it strikes the floor.
A fall still broke not; but the words inked strong and soar.
While we are a result of a fatal accident called birth,
One has to live long enough on this earth;

Till we emerge and our souls turn into the stardust,
Away from earthly envies, vanity and lust.
The Silence before the first ray of the sun,
Silenced! How many such Red would die?
Silenced! Standing tall for justice, but gain none.
Though silenced! It's all a fabricated flak and lie.

So could we be silenced from the east to west?
From the north to the south and beyond. No!
The sun would yet again rise with a roar like a beast.
To out power the rogues and set the country aglow.
Or you would see the river and the oceans weep,
For all of us to be silenced forever in just one sweep.
Shush....

Sir Stalin

Whate'er be the earthly doom,
He bequeathed in solitude,
Let forgo the family in bloom.
He wanted not, scale great altitude,
Neither did he want solace,
Nor stars did he pursue,
But he who is Stalin ended novice;
At Bangalore to a rag pickers crew.
In a murky torn garb, he picked up dirt.
Smelled of stale yet paid no heed,
To the old neighbourhood or hurt.
Inaudible yet steady did his deed.
From what people deem, you leapt
And spake the English tongue.
Caressing the dogs with whom he slept,
Did give a damn whether he was old or young.
Stalin, he did really live for real,
Away from the desirous reel.
A family of envious breed,
He did not astray life or plead.
Whate'er be the earthly doom,
He bequeathed in solitude,
Had I been the queen or the King,
I would have knighted him Sir.
For rendering noble services in kind.
The one who truly deserve to be dined,
With the queen and king like mind.
The one who should be Ashir,
The one who is Sir Stalin.

Soul of a Bottled Genie

In a poignant fable,
Once lived a genie.
Trapped in a glass bottle,
Caught unaware of the horizon;
His cosmic powers never unleashed.

Man, A self-devouring creature,
Captured the genius genie within.
Genie cried!
A little pearl of tear;
Dripped unto the bottom.

A disguised master – Society
At times, family at times,
Friends at times, fear at times,
Kept the bottle of illusion at place.
Genie cried!
A little of pearl of tear,
Dripped unto the bottom.

Oh Benevolent! Bail me out!
Let me unleash the powers,
And grant you three wishes.
Genie cried!
A little pearl of tear,
Dripped unto the bottom.

Knights marched deaf,
Used human shields.
Pundits lost their purpose;
Statesman, fascist alike
Laws of hell they brought unto earth.
Genie cried!
A little pearl of tear,
Dripped unto the bottom.

Finally a poet sang,
The song of the genie.
Thou'Art he scribbled;
On the bottle.
The rallying cry echoed!
Far across the mountains,
Across the oceans,
For months and for years,
But none did open the bottle.
Genie cried!
A pearl of tear,
Dripped unto the bottom.

Genie sank in his tears.
Statesman saw the bottle of pearls,
Broke open to find;
his tormented soul
Flicker through space
Unto eternity.
The soul of a bottled genie.

I AM THE PUGILIST

When my destiny started haunting me,
I turned into a pugilist
A pugilist who is always the victim of betrayal,
A pugilist who is the victim of love,
Victim of friendship.

When my destiny started haunting me,
I turned into a pugilist
A pugilist to fight for justice,

When this world now,
Is governed not by god,
A pugilist was born,
A pugilist to fight for victory,

A pugilist who can see the future so promising.
When my destiny started haunting me
I turned into a pugilist.
A pugilist who burned himself,
In the inferno of his anger.
A pugilist for the poor and the needed,
A pugilist for the world and now
I am the pugilist

Endeavour and Escapism

In search of my destiny,
I started off
The beginning of a new endeavour
I was carried away Enthusiasm and proactiveness
Supported me a long way
So far the wind blew in the right direction
Climate changed abruptly
I ended up in a cyclone hit area
My legs now tremble and
Hesitate to go ahead
I was stabbed on my back
An act of cowardice
My opposition now being so strong
My legs now tremble
And hesitate to go ahead
I tend to adopt strategies of an escapist
Deep inside I can hear
My conscience utter the words of optimism
Far away my destiny beckons me
I can see the future
So bright and prosperous
Never again shall my legs tremble
And hesitate to go ahead
And my conscience keeps me on the go

God is one for all

Jesus, Krishna, Allah thou different names,
Love is god and not god is love.
Religion no bar, caste no bar
There is only one god and that is love
Oh mighty souls on earth promote love and not god.
Promote love and not thy name
Discriminate not! The people, on Gods

For God is one for all.
Teach them to love,
Teach them to be friends,
Teach them to serve the world,

Teach them not theology,
Teach them not to discriminate each other,
On the basis of thy name.
Oh mighty souls on earth promote love
And not God, for God is one for all.

The Curse

Infuriating pain,
Illuminated the road to wisdom
He the heavenly father showered love
Like rain during mid-summer
The first bud sprouted in the garden
Thus spreading effervescence of hope
Though birth neither death did
Stop to the forces of mankind
Nor did the mid-summer rain succeed
Great devastations as a result of economics
The world yet is to witness
Thus is the ill fate
The incurable curse of Kali
Adulterated fruits of the farm
Could only be the greatest disrespect
Shown to the mother
Thus making the curse irrevocable
The more you make infertile the soil,
We witness infertile mankind
Adulterated fruits of the farm
Thus produce adulterated minds
Numerous killings result in slaughtering
Limited not just to cattle

But the throat slitting reality
Spread among us, would
Thus a man kill and eat another
A day marked the darkest in history
Would finally seek the end
The brightest star out there
Would close his eyes
Covering those gleaming light on us
Thus would leave us in the darkness for eternity
The mortals would perish
But you and I the good souls
Would yet lead us to light
A bright new star, a bright new world.

Identity

Frozen between time and space
Lost in natures concentration camp
I had to forgo my identity by face
Religion, caste and creed, what a shamp?

With several identities while I fiddle
It looks like an epic, this riddle
Narrated with elegance and style
The fable takes you far a mile

For reasons beyond imagination,
Fanatic emotions sprout as instigators;
And kill the mocking bird of the nation,
Ensuing in blown up crime indicators.

Shackled in chains and caned,
My heart would still pray for peace.
Break my physique until you have drained,
Yet my mind is free to think in solace.

Ways of life, obscure and esoteric,
In search of thy identity mesmeric.
A warrior, a poet, a teacher at times
Changing to meet and keep up with times.

The law of the land fierce and vicious
Tiring strive and remorse delicious
Bitter enough to chew or to bite
To be able to swallow nor to spit

Identity thus cause hassle galore,
Do away with one for the daily chore;
For I have to return to his abode,
Once over with this part or episode.

Identity
Frozen between time and space
Lost in natures concentration camp
I had to forgo my identity by face
Religion, caste and creed.
What a shamp?
with several identities
while I fiddle. it looks
like an epic.
this riddle

Clowns Abode

A boat apropos to life,
Rocks in the insatiable storm,
Like a piercing knife,
Droplets fall unto us, warm.

The heavens agony pouring,
Tides in the ocean soaring,
New highs to rattle the boat.
Yet does grapple to keep afloat.

Balancing act on a thin rope,
Battling the inevitable on hope,
Annihilation of ourselves amidst;
Growth is infallible on him to forbid.

The smiles and frowns,
On the faces of the clowns;
Alight on applause galore;
But still bleed sorrow oneself for.

What for, for this is momentary,
Life transforms into different forms.
Those good ones into a fairy,
And the rest to daemons as are the norms.

Resist not to laugh on oneself,
Would help one to be an elf;
After life, but for now bowed,
He is laughing at the clowns abode.

The Wall

I am shunned within the four wall,
Of caste, creed, religion, and capitalism;
Neither big nor too small,
I too am a soul; a kind of an organism.

As dawn brought the golden rays of the sun,
Inducing new life into the flesh, blood, and the spirit;
Yet, I am still confined within; thy cursed son.
Confined of nature or to relish your merit.

Despite abundance beneath the ocean,
In the skies, across the land of dreams
Wonder! What a sight of Joy? An emotion;
Yet I am, still shunned in the tears; a stream.

Blinded by vision, emptiness in my soul,
The silence of my heart shrieks at thou;
Yearning for thy love; served in a bowl.
Had the gentle breeze soothed my skin in lieu?

Breach those unconscious walls, nonsense;
Not by vision, but blinded by conscious,
Arouse the soul at night in the presence of the moon
Keep moving on, Break those walls; cocoon.

Poverty

A poor family dwell in the slum,
A life desolate in swamp and in despair.
They wished for food not a cake; plum,
A mud pot; lay empty never afire.

Their fable unfair of betrayal,
Rich gloated over their failure for survival.
Thy lord showered misfortune,
Like a rainstorm, upon them in tune.

Shrunken clothes and sullen eyes,
Wrinkled faces, forgotten; lost a smile;
When did we hear last, their cries?
Their countless fatalities; a closed file.

I wish all the rich in this land,
Become beggars in a no man's land.
Destitute of bread and water; fractionate;
So they learn to be compassionate.

Let go crumbling for their careless thoughts,
Lay them to rest; cold in mud and dust.
Loyalty to be learned among rest of the lots,
The poor and the needy; serve them just.

MYOPIA

I met this man from a distant land,
Short! Shorter than a normal one;
Masculine chest and frisky forehand,
He could turn a visible midnight sun.

In bright daylight, he brought darkness,
Unto earth; covering o'er love with hate.
Murmur did spread; life's harshness
Like a wildfire did decide their fate.

Hammered and chained, the little ones,
Not to spare their wards as well and nuns,
Massacred one by one, and blood they sip,
Ruthless daemons above all sportsmanship.

Did threw their spears, bodies with it ripped,
Heavens did weep with tears they dripped;
Oh lord! What heart they have, did it beat?
What Dreadful hand and so as their feet?

Fry their brains in a furnace, how?
Show us a weakness, as we bow
Fight them eye to eye! The lord murmured
For the daemon cannot see afar blurred.

The short man hopped up high in defence,
But the sword did shed blood, cut him into two
The rest ran and jumped o'er the fence
Love did return to the land in due.

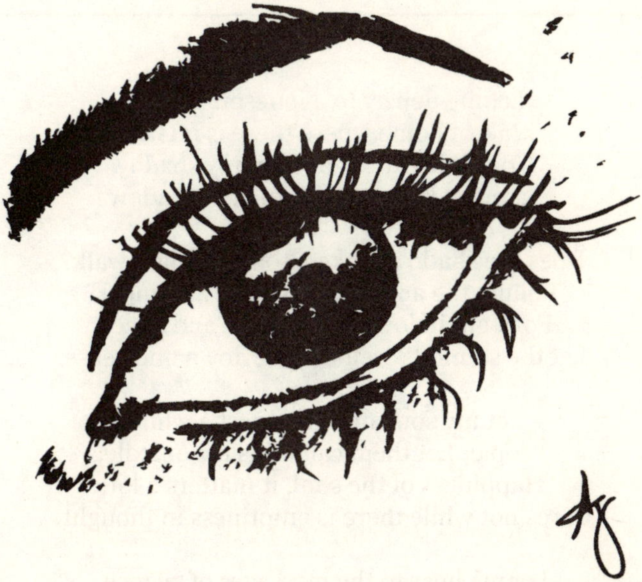

Silence

Let me depart to a lonesome place.
Make a home where there is no face,
No neighbours, not even my shadow
Paradise like, let it be such a meadow.

Does the shadow make a sound while I walk?
Pollute the ambience in mute and mock.
For I am in love with silence and peace,
Let the sound therefore tone down and cease.

Let my soul and mind rest a while.
People; Let them call it insane or exile,
Happiness of the soul, it matters a lot;
Cares not while there is emptiness in thought.

Let me hear to the messages of silence,
Let the world oust me! As the price of defiance.
I shall neither grumble nor crave,
Much worthier to live; least not like a slave.

Depth

Deep inside, I searched for a soul,
But it was all a rut and foul.
Craving for the stench of her flesh,
There wasn't love, just lust afresh.

The world stripped her bit by bit,
That included everyone else and me.
Penetrating her vagina deeper slit,
Bereft emotion lifeless flesh there lie.

There is an emptiness after pleasure,
A little illicit intimate act of leisure.
What have I gained thus, Is it Joy?
Victim of addictive ecstasy, thy clay toy.

I lay still, trying to peep deep inside
Emptiness, the mystery of depth
My craving for purpose, let fate it decide
Life unwrapped, empty unto death.

Sync with the Poet

Sync with the beat of my heart,
And fall in love like a poet.
As he splits the world a half part,
The one filled with love is the kismet,
And he slaughters agony with his words;
Fly to the heaven like the birds.
Flap the wings; sync it with my heart.
Elevate the wisdom you impart,
through my words, a class apart
Play it to the tunes of Mozart,
Until you rejoice in the Love of Gods.

Unmindful

Unmindful of the time,
I wander in vain with no goal set,
As the crimson red sun set,
At dusk, I had lost all that was prime.

DRUNKARD

Ecstasy, The other name for wine!
Pour it to life, let the world dine.

It's the creator's splendid drink,
Let me revel in this drunken frenzy

Pour it in words; to a reader's merry,
And it will split open the door to the legendary.

Section 5: Nature

Sundari

Mystique of nature; the beautiful ones,
Sundari! The queen of the swamp in the Sundarbans,
And in my home town an old market place,
She grew dense with virtue and grace.
Coast, where the river meets the Arabian Sea.
Mangroves flourished forever in glee.
Trifling touch of the tinkling tides tickle the root,
The wind chimes, and the hustling leaves, Mangroves;
Make a home to Fluttering birds pretty and cute,
Making it indeed a nature's treasure-trove.
The fireflies alight the creek at night,
And the gurgling water reflect her charm in twilight.
The striped monstrous cats, the endangered Tiger,
Occasionally roars past the shallow bay.
While one or two evil men pull the trigger,
Then there he would on a muddy bloody lay,
In tranquil, his soul would escape gravity,
A life lost for the evil fella's false vanity.
Sundari weeps while her near and dear,
Has fallen prey to the man and out of fear,
She weeps further waiting to be conserved.
While the good ones hop forward to preserve,
Capitalist would turn rebel, who? The real terror.
He would then think how to use?
How to use, the mangrove forest with no error
With no error, a man can only think how to use?
How to use the Sundari? How to use whate'er?

THE BESIEGED SCION!

Oh! Dear Parijata, the besieged scion
Of the trees celestial, enthroned like the Lion,
Of the Jungle, the emperor of nature,
Will you ever again sprout in the future?

Have I not stayed awake in the night?
To watch your coral jasmine bloom,
The tree of sorrow, queen of the night
Alas! Who had left you so gloom?

Voluptuously you open at dusk,
Encompassing your fragrance so contiguous
Melting even the valiant heart with the tusk
Why do you then fall by dawn conspicuous?

Born out of ashes, your love for the sun,
Never could the heart be won.
Woe thus caused by the sunset yesteryear,
Is that why your flower shed like a tear?

Once Kṛṣṇá off rooted you from the heaven
Fierce battle fought with Indra though
He planted you on Satyabhama's haven
Hence you are the blessed krsna's bestow

Yet you grew oblique and shed
Your flowers at Rukmini's abode
She did adore in her garden the flower bed
Thus Annoying Satyabhama's curse you owed

Is that why your flowers shed at sunrise?
Bees and butterflies with feet did the magic
Fruit you bear like a heart, sprout at highs
Though life enthralled of despair and tragic.

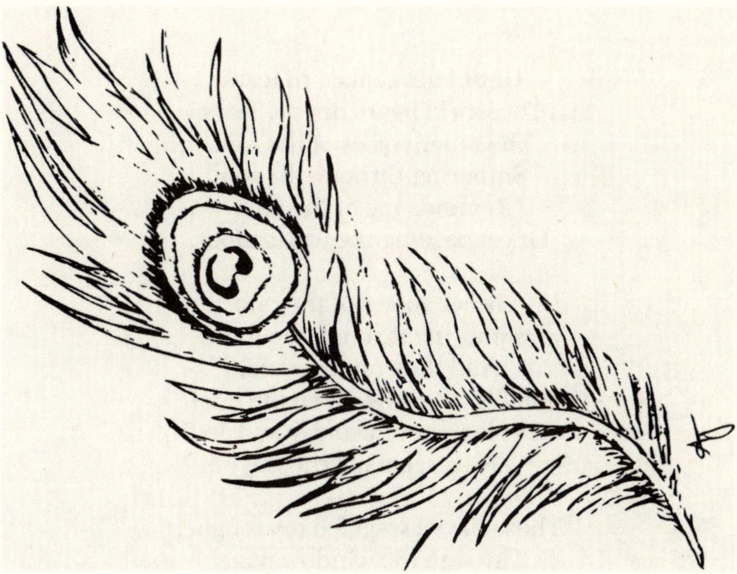

The Sky

Until I get soaked in tears,
The world hears not my fears.
The inner voices of the rain,
Slithering through the roof
Reminds me of the pain,
Of yet battling the world aloof.

Inner voices of the rain
Slithering through the roof,
And then on the pane,
Finally touching down the hoof,
An element of wonder and Joy
Now seems like a ploy

Those days I waggled my tongue,
Through the window pane.
Would then take a plunge,
Swaying to the melody of rain,
Merry; till dragged to the courtyard,
Furious and worried motherly guard.

Shower, Shower, Shower
Shower all your mighty power
Did I not grew up with your touch
Tender and with love so much
Then, it was never your tears
Neither did I have any fears

Wonder why now shower tears
Afar from the sky of fairies
Inner voices of the rain
Thy voice reverberate in my ears
Bringing alone the pain
Unto earth for several years

Knock off those cruel adult,
Upon natures will; to catapult.
Inner voices of the rain,
Now seems like a feign,
Of adversity and slain,
Showering from the sky of pain.

Shower, Shower, Shower
Shower it like blessing
Shower all your mighty power
Unto earth till redressing
Hear not my fear,
Until we the people smear.

Shower it from the sky of pain.

Nilgiris

Of world's greatest wonders,
Do count the Blue Mountains of Nilgiris,
A symbolic rendezvous of the heaven;
And the earth, a paradise for the mortals haven,
In the skies among the angels of Gods.
Thy beauty invoke the poet in me,
Delight me more and cleanse my heart,
Pure; No light but for the smiling moon,
Makes the darkness visible; the sights of joy,
So high in bliss, I do sing your heavenly muse.
Winter clouds; chilling breeze brushed my face,
The heavenly kiss of a peaceful night,
With chirping sparrows and cricket galore;
The silence of the woods, is beauty indescribable.
From a distance, I yonder, ponder and wonder;
What made you the Paradise on earth?

Venus

The beauty of the night skies,
The planet of love, your twinkle;
Emanates blue rays of love,
Unto the earth from heaven.
I lay quietly on my back
Gazing at your beauty.
Romancing the goddess of love,
Tasting the nectar of your flowers
Only to spread love, what form it may be,
To fill this world with love and peace.
Our moon has stains, but not a
Single stain in your love so pure.
You tie our hearts together
In a single twain, the lovers twain.
I have known not any bitterness
When I pray at your temple,
The largest and the most splendid.
Allow me to kiss, thy cheeks
Because there is in love, I;
Thy insane eternal lover.

Section 6: Death

Ecstasy

In ecstasy of our identity and pride,
People of thy kingdom; gust!
In control of all the power eyed,
We wander with greed and lust.

Wonder why? This rally to the crest.
Does it signify any purpose to the guest?
A temporary dweller on this land,
Drunken frenzy, fiery and grand.

Like the dying wick in the lamp,
We burn aglow like an inferno,
Only to realise that it's a shamp;
Beyond the wisdom we know.

Crushing several innocent lives,
When we at last reach the crest;
There is none to share those vibes,
Cos one has to, alone eternal rest,
In his arms forever in harmony.

Lay me to rest

Lay me to rest,
As this isn't a place for me.
Drown me to death,
In the river, besides her I was born.
Let me find solace,
In her bosom and suckle her breast again.
Like a child innocent and forever rejoice.
Once again allow me to relive those days,
Just before my eyes are shut in eternity;
For my soul is immortal like none.
And let the world bashful, burn into ashes,
In the flicker of my soul.
Lay me to rest.

Farmers Death

I will mourn not your death,
Cause you only existed in words
For your silence has murdered
Many innocent lives, precious.
In the stillness of time, that refuses to pass by
A poet's hope beyond life and death,
Conjures democracy like never before.
The wake of a new era is calling,
The silent commune of writers,
Lift thy, mighty fallen pen
And ink using the darkest of red,
Viscous blood to avoid many more
Shredding of life, in the name of the fallen kingdom.
The peasants of the land, lay still
Mother mourns, Father mourns, and Brother mourns,
The entire Nation mourns, the death of a farmer.
I will mourn not your death.
The writer is silent. I believe it is the real death.
The death of a mankind in the silence of a pen.
I mourn silence over the death of a farmer.

The dead man's Soul

I wake up again in the dark
Surrounded by the wooden walls
Of a coffin buried in a park
Next to the legendary great falls
I cry all night in vain
For I am afraid of the dark
I hear children play in merry
With their wards on their sides
And I smell golden lily
The flower of death
Why haunt the dead? I ask!
For I am already decaying
Beneath this beautiful park.
Do one a thing for my soul,
Cut a hole next to my grave,
For my soul entrapped,
Would let go in the skies blue.
Or I shall be a wanderlust
In the forbidden world for the dead.

Loss

I had a little home here,
Its long back, I fear.
If that time had come again,
I wish. Bringing along the pain,
Of memories so sweet.

Traveller

In the greenest of the valleys
I wander like a nomad
In the gushing blue waters,
I sail through like Columbus
Listening to the inside of nature
The outside of nature, listening to the birds,
The wild, the beauty and my inner self.
Listening to the sound of peace, I find solace;
Away from the sound of guns that
Gutter through the air, killing.
Killing a man, a woman;
Killing an innocent child;
Killing anything and everything, even a dragonfly.
Caught in between time and space,
I too am relative. A relative of nature.
I can hear myself, I can hear the morning,
The noon and the dusk.
I can hear the flowers bloom and die.
I can hear the weep of a mother, a child and a father.
I can hear the roar of the wild,
I can feel the depth of the wound,
I can hear the nature cry,
For peace, for solace.
I can also hear my soul
Flicker through the skies.
Traveling through the earth
Is the most horrendous experience.

